Ask And You Shall Receive

Inspiration Notebook

"**Ask**, and it will be given to you; **seek** and you will find; **knock** and the door will be opened to you. For everyone who asks receives; the one who seeks finds; and to the one who knocks, the door will be opened."

—Matthew 7:7-8 (NIV)

This Inspiration Notebook belongs to and is prayed over

By: _____   Date: _____

Rediscover Truth

Ask And You Shall Receive
Inspiration Notebook
Receive Joy

Receive Joy Publishing
Naples, Florida, U.S.A.

© 2020 Receive Joy
Carisa Jones, Sylvia Lehmann
All rights reserved.
Cover photography by Deborah W. Maurer © 2017

ISBN: 978-0-9988484-5-7

Receive Joy, LLC
www.receivejoy.com
ask@receivejoy.com

YOUR GUIDE FOR USING THE INSPIRATION NOTEBOOK

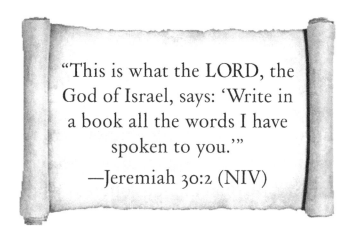

"This is what the LORD, the God of Israel, says: 'Write in a book all the words I have spoken to you.'"
—Jeremiah 30:2 (NIV)

Now that you have read *Ask And You Shall Receive* by Receive Joy, let us put the Nine Step Method into daily action. Receive Joy designed this *Inspiration Notebook* as a platform to create and record your inspirations, insights, goals, and daily highlights. Inspirational daily writing enables you to experience a purposeful life with clarity. Your plans of action, written insights, and creative thoughts direct you toward your goals and keep you focused on your target.

This annual journal allows you to start journaling any day of the year.

The purpose of the *Ask And You Shall Receive Inspiration Notebook* is to have all inspired thoughts and positive words collected, organized, and recorded in one place. This helps raise your awareness and provides an organized platform to consciously create in writing your positive, happy, light, and easy life.

Let our *Inspiration Notebook* assist you in imagining, creating, recording, and remembering your miraculous life. This notebook is a tool to help you measure your continual growth and accomplishments.

 Now pick up a pen, and script your life in your own hand.

Start by filling in your **Divine Mission Statement**. What is your life about? Include your key values and words that describe you. Revisit and rewrite your Mission Statement as often as you desire.

Next, fill in your **Goals For This Year**. What do you wish to accomplish during the next 365 days? By signing the page, you consciously commit to a contract with yourself. This is an opportunity to hold yourself accountable to the standards and goals you call in. You may choose to obtain a second signature from your prayer/accountability partner.

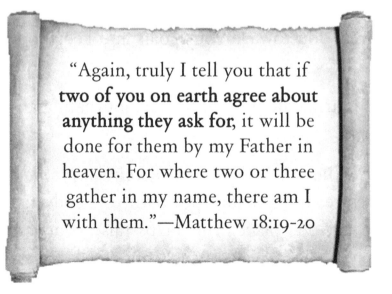

"Again, truly I tell you that if **two of you on earth agree about anything they ask for,** it will be done for them by my Father in heaven. For where two or three gather in my name, there am I with them."—Matthew 18:19-20

Out of your list of goals, pick the most important one. To keep your eyes on the victory, write your goal in the center of the bull's-eye on the **Focus Target** page. Fill in your additional goals according to their importance in the outer rings. After you have filled in the whole target, make a copy and place the sheet where it can be seen daily.

Simultaneously, it is beneficial to have goals in all important areas of your life. Live by design and fill in the rings of the eight Focus Targets following your GOALS FOR THIS YEAR-Target to enhance your clarity and focus. What are your ideals when it comes to these eight valuable areas:

- ♥ Happiness
- ♥ Health
- ♥ Wealth
- ♥ Love & Community
- ♥ Growth
- ♥ Spirituality
- ♥ Career
- ♥ Personal Space

We provided you with an overview of the **Nine Steps** to consciously create. Each month starts with a summary of a lesson as presented in *Ask And You Shall Receive*, followed by the opportunity to express your **Gratitude** and give thanks for the **Blessings** you have already **received**. This builds your faith and instills confidence that we can achieve everything with God. Each of us has accomplished so much already. See your whole life as a blessing. Practicing gratitude moves us into the matching state to continue receiving.

Next, we choose our **Monthly Goals** from our Yearly Goals. We further divide them up into **Weekly Goals** to allow for easy success with achievable steps to focus on. During the month, you might wish to fill in the section **Gains, Successes, and Miracles Received**. Thus, you'll have a monthly overview to refer back to in the years to come to remember the highlights of your year. Henceforth, your accomplished goals will become your next month's gratitude.

Read the daily inspiration and receive joy. Be blessed with fresh inspiration for your day. You might wish to write the day of the week next to the date.

The daily pages may be used in different ways. Receive Joy suggests to use the lined space to journal:

- ♥ The inspired thoughts you received during daily meditation
- ♥ Write down your first thought that came to you when sitting in quiet contemplation
- ♥ Your prayers

- ♥ The goodness you choose to remember from this day
- ♥ What you are grateful for today
- ♥ What brought you joy
- ♥ Insights of the day
- ♥ What you learned today
- ♥ List your accomplishments
- ♥ The Bible verse you cherish today and your thoughts on it. There is a Bible verse provided at the end of each month. You may wish to start with this verse
- ♥ An act of kindness you received today and how you brought light and love to someone else's day

Tape notes, photos, business cards, and other memorabilia such as theater tickets and stickers in your journal. At the end of the journal, there are blank pages for **Notes** included to give you ample space for additional thoughts and inspirations.

Take time to journal each day. Once filled in, this book becomes your life's diary to refer back to and remember each step of your way. In the years to come, your journals will amount to a treasure you have fun referring back to. The collection of your journals are a joyful record of a life well lived to share with your family and friends. Write the year on the spine and save them on your bookshelf—each is a chapter in the book of your life!

> "May He give you the desire of your heart and make all your plans succeed."
> —Proverbs 16:3 (NIV)

To God be the glory!

With Love and Gratitude,

Receive Joy

Rediscover Truth

MY DIVINE MISSION

Write down your divine mission and life's purpose to be constantly aware of it. In case you are still searching for your life's mission, take the time right now to define yourself. Refer to pages 149 to 154 of the book *Ask And You Shall Receive* by Receive Joy to help you find your purpose. We came into this awesome world filled with love and now we are here with the opportunity to experience this love and light for ourselves and to share it with others.

My divine mission is _____

_____

_____

_____

_____

_____

_____

_____

_____

_____

_____

GOALS FOR THIS YEAR

_____

I vividly see myself with my goals obtained and miracles created!

_____   _____
Signature   Date

GOALS FOR THIS YEAR _____

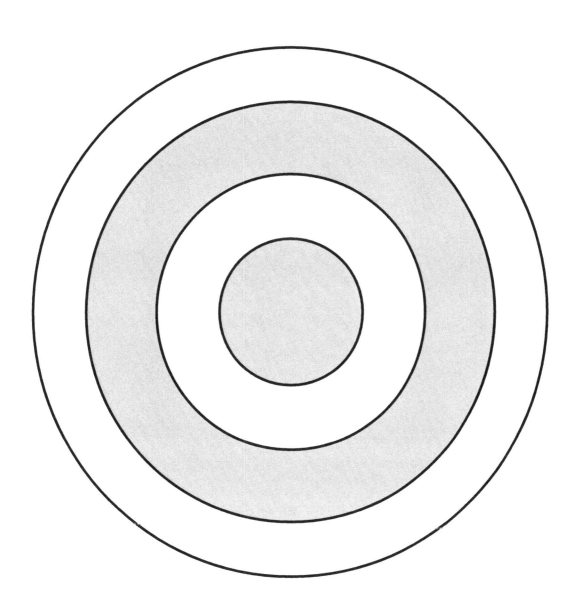

HAPPINESS

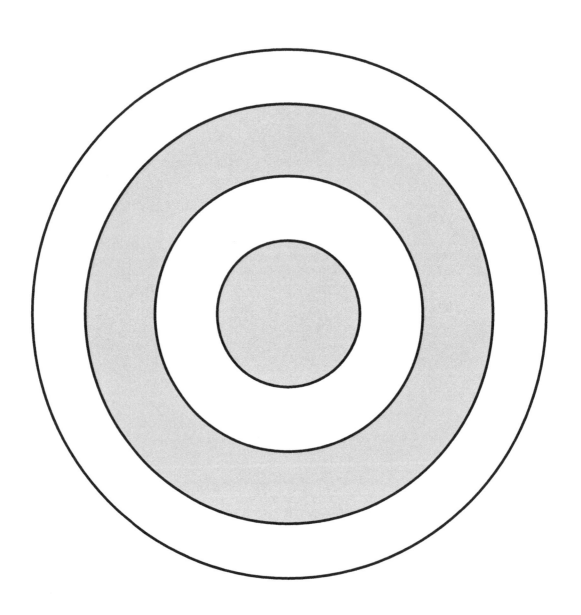

HEALTH

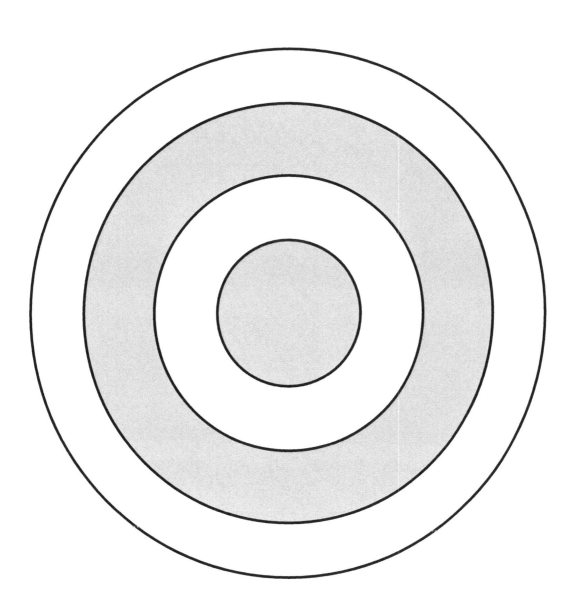

WEALTH

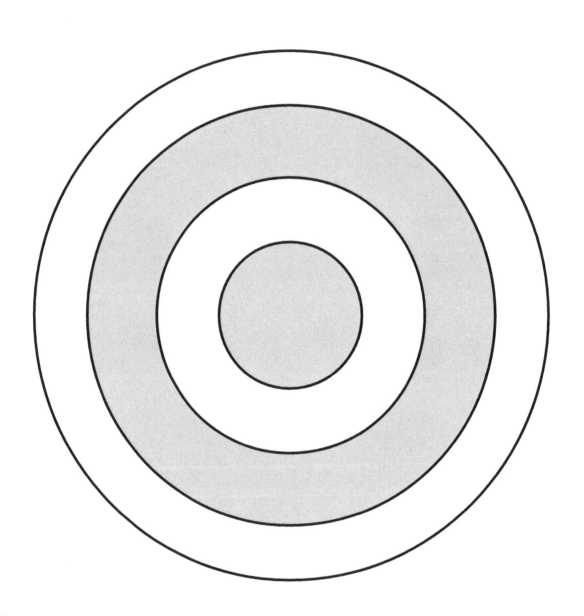

LOVE & COMMUNITY

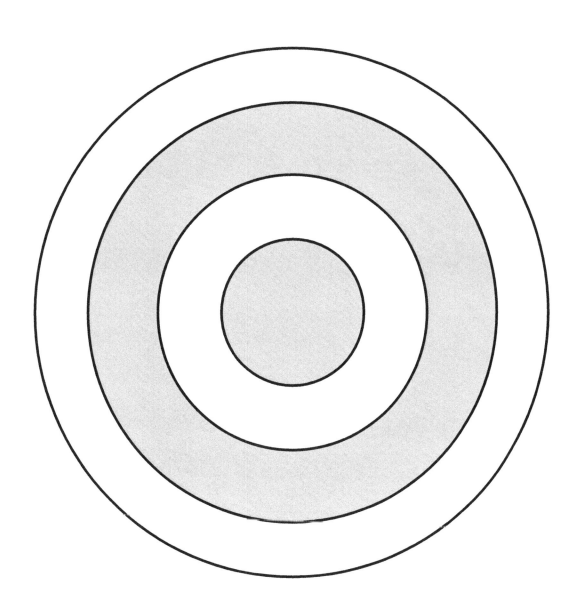

GROWTH

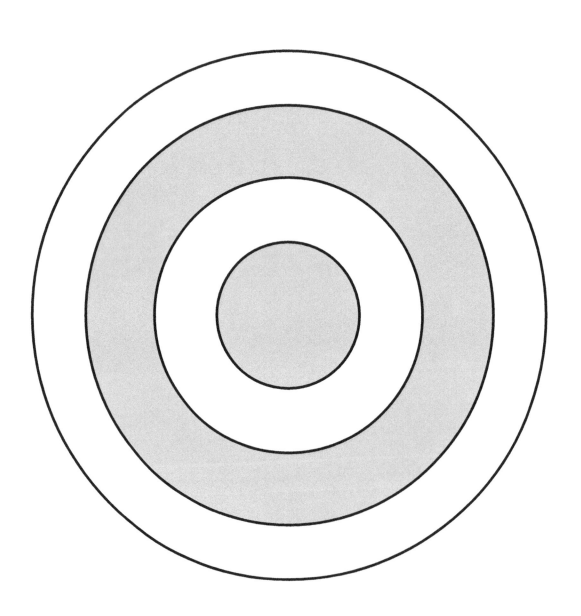

SPIRITUALITY

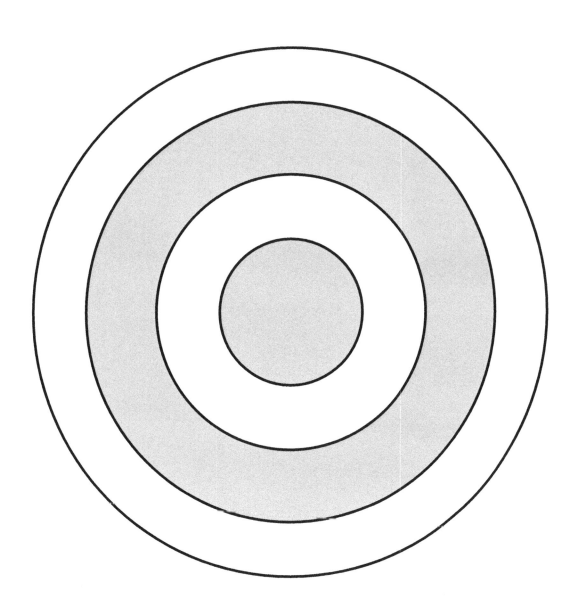

CAREER

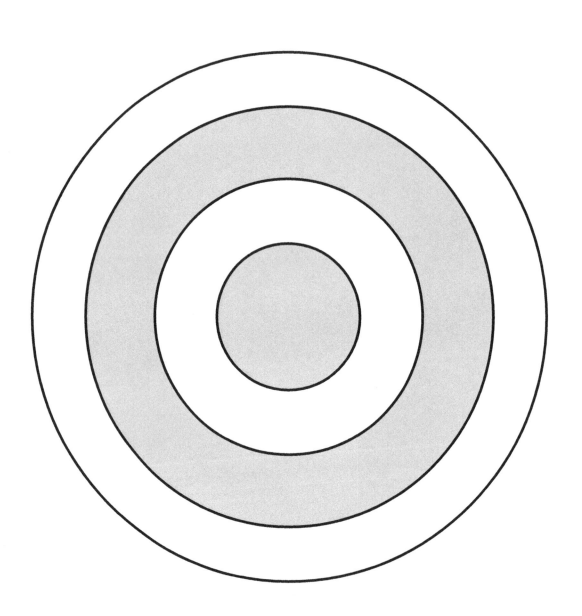

PERSONAL SPACE

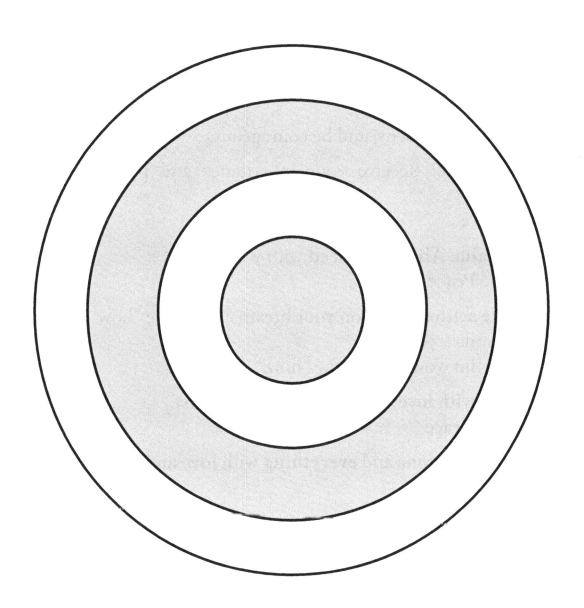

THE NINE STEPS TO CONSCIOUS CREATION

1. **Connect**: Plug into God's Almighty **Gift**, the Power of the Universe, and discover your life's purpose.

2. **Declare**: Be clear about what you are truly seeking and ask for it.
   Have **Faith,** focus, and be courageous.

3. **Dominate**: Receive your inheritance and put on your crown.
   Believe.

4. **Be calm**: **Align** your head with your heart.
   Have **Peace**.

5. **Take action**: Focus on your breath and let the "how" be up to God.
   Let Him wow us with the "how." He does it.

6. **Lead with love**: Let us **love ourselves first**.
   Have **Grace**.

7. **Bless everyone** and **everything** with **love and gratitude.**
   Have **Mercy**.

8. **Expect the miracle in every moment**. Know the **Truth**.
   Be conscious of what you create and allow yourself to receive your desires.

9. **Have fun and celebrate**: Enjoy your creation and rejoice.
   Trust God.

THE POWER OF STARTING NEW

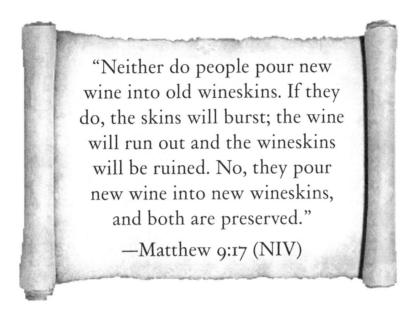

"Neither do people pour new wine into old wineskins. If they do, the skins will burst; the wine will run out and the wineskins will be ruined. No, they pour new wine into new wineskins, and both are preserved."
—Matthew 9:17 (NIV)

Let us constantly choose to let the past be just that and let each new moment be our NOW—a new experience full of possibilities.

Every day is new. We are new every moment. We are new wineskins when we allow God's light to flow through us. We choose to see the perfection in ourselves and everyone else just as we are in this very moment. Let our minds be open, calm, and relaxed. He desires us to be a new wineskin and be ready and willing to accept the new wine that He offers. Our new wineskin is our new and fresh awareness.

Let us shed yesterday's beliefs and continue to script our life in greatness.

JANUARY

GRATITUDE AND BLESSINGS RECEIVED

JANUARY

MONTHLY GOALS

_____
_____
_____
_____
_____
_____
_____
_____
_____
_____
_____
_____
_____

GAINS, SUCCESSES, AND MIRACLES RECEIVED

_____
_____
_____
_____
_____
_____
_____
_____
_____
_____

JANUARY

WEEKLY GOALS

Week 1

_____
_____
_____
_____
_____
_____

Week 2

_____
_____
_____
_____
_____
_____

Week 3

_____
_____
_____
_____
_____
_____

Week 4

_____
_____
_____
_____
_____
_____

JANUARY

1 *I now joyfully accept and appreciate the abundant life the Universe offers me.*

2 *I am in perfect health. My body feels amazing.*

3 *I accept all the good around me.*

4 *I flow with all that life offers me in every moment.*

JANUARY

5 *I write my thoughts, desires, and dreams down on paper. I journal.*

6 *I choose to feel excellent about myself. I make this choice every morning.*

7 *There is only happiness. I rejoice always.*

8 *My perfect life is full of abundance. I recognize abundance everywhere. I tap into all the abundance.*

JANUARY

9 *I am full of energy. I have the energy of a child.*

10 *Ideas come to me from everywhere.*

11 *I allow peace within me and in my environment.*

12 *I choose to see the good in all.*

JANUARY

13 *I am happy to be me.*

14 *I smile, laugh, and dance.*

15 *I am living a life of abundance, happiness, and wealth.*

16 *I am thrilled and filled with rejuvenating, revitalizing life.*

JANUARY

17   *I show gratitude and thanksgiving every day.*

18   *I respond to myself and others with kindness.*

19   *Today I breathe new life into my goals and desires.*

20   *I love my life and I do great things that I find fun.*

JANUARY

21 *Grace, mercy, and peace are with me.*

22 *I am so grateful that I am part of the wonderful abundance that all humanity comes from.*

23 *My body uses relaxation as a method to rejuvenate.*

24 *I create miracles in every moment.*

JANUARY

25 *I allow God's goodness to flow through me.*

26 *I visualize my perfect life.*

27 *I am amazing.*

28 *I understand that this life was given to me to be joyful and to celebrate.*

JANUARY

29 *My fun brings all the wealth I desire.*

30 *My skin glows. I have full, thick, and healthy hair.*

31 *I accept all truth and all understanding.*

> "For My yoke is **easy**, and My load is **light**."
> —Matthew 11:30
> (NASB)

THE POWER OF THE UNIVERSE

> "**Ask**, and it will be given to you; **seek** and you will find; **knock** and the door will be opened to you. For everyone who asks receives; the one who seeks finds; and to the one who knocks, the door will be opened."
>
> —Matthew 7:7-8 (NIV)

When God flung the stars into existence, He set up a divine delivery system. Since we are His most valued creation, He wishes for us to be aware of it, understand it, access it, communicate with it, and use it in our daily lives for our greatest good. It is always fully available to us. There is more than enough of everything for everyone. There is absolute abundance.

Let us decide to open ourselves and our lives to receive. Ask, Seek, Knock!

FEBRUARY

GRATITUDE AND BLESSINGS RECEIVED

FEBRUARY

MONTHLY GOALS

_____

GAINS, SUCCESSES, AND MIRACLES RECEIVED

_____

FEBRUARY

WEEKLY GOALS

Week 1

Week 2

Week 3

Week 4

FEBRUARY

1 *My perfect life is full of peaceful energy.*

2 *My day is all planned out the night before. I know my next step.*

3 *I love myself. I am beautiful.*

4 *I remain cheerful so that I can best serve myself and others.*

FEBRUARY

5 *Wealth continually flows to me. I love being rich.*

6 *All my cells are happy and healthy.*

7 *I am the co-creator of my own life and I act with grace and mercy in all I do.*

8 *I joyfully allow all that is good in.*

FEBRUARY

9 *I know that everything I focus on I receive more of.*

10 *I find it easy to love myself and others.*

11 *I am a rejoicing soul.*

12 *I have all the resources I desire. I am resourceful.*

FEBRUARY

13   *I am aligned with the energy of abundance.*

_____
_____
_____
_____
_____

14   *My life continues to be better and better. I focus on the greater good.*

_____
_____
_____
_____
_____

15   *My life is light and easy.*

_____
_____
_____
_____
_____

16   *I am in charge of my thoughts.*

_____
_____
_____
_____
_____

FEBRUARY

17 *I commit to be love; I am love.*

18 *I choose to bring joy into every situation of my life.*

19 *I am successful. I surround myself with amazing, successful people.*

20 *I am happy and active.*

FEBRUARY

21 *I am grateful that I am living my divine mission.*

22 *I am fulfilled. I know that my desires are taken care of.*

23 *I only speak positive and loving words. I know my words create everything.*

24 *Divine love attracts all good.*

FEBRUARY

25 *I make sure I am having fun every day.*

26 *I am open and receptive to all the wealth in the Universe.*

27 *I smile constantly.*

28 *Each day I create greatness.*

FEBRUARY

29   *Miracles flow to me continually.*

_____
_____
_____
_____
_____
_____

"I tell you the truth, anyone who believes in me will **do the same works I have done, and even greater works**, because I am going to be with the Father."

—John 14:12 (NLT)

THE POWER OF USING POSITIVE WORDS AS A BLESSING

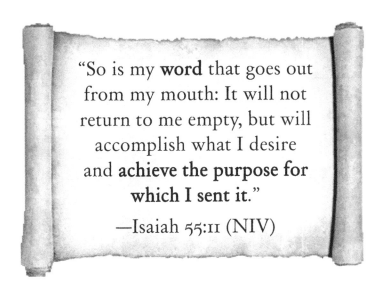

"So is my **word** that goes out from my mouth: It will not return to me empty, but will accomplish what I desire and **achieve the purpose for which I sent it.**"

—Isaiah 55:11 (NIV)

Every word is a creation. We can choose to create love, joy, gratitude, hope, compassion, mercy, praise, and much more positivity with our words—or we can choose to create the lack thereof. Are our words supporting our purpose?

Let us be conscious of which words we send out to achieve what we desire. Write them down and let us edit our words three times!

MARCH

GRATITUDE AND BLESSINGS RECEIVED

MARCH

MONTHLY GOALS

___

GAINS, SUCCESSES, AND MIRACLES RECEIVED

___

MARCH

WEEKLY GOALS

Week 1
_____
_____
_____
_____
_____
_____

Week 2
_____
_____
_____
_____
_____
_____

Week 3
_____
_____
_____
_____
_____
_____

Week 4
_____
_____
_____
_____
_____
_____

MARCH

1 *I am a true blessing.*

2 *I believe in my dreams. I follow my dreams. My dreams all come true.*

3 *I allow my love to flow freely. My supply of love is abundant.*

4 *I am grateful for this perfect day.*

MARCH

5 *I allow money to flow joyfully and freely into my life.*

6 *I take care of my body. I eat nourishing foods and drink pure water.*

7 *I know what I desire.*

8 *I am completely calm and at peace.*

MARCH

9 *I can do anything and everything with God.*

10 *I am worthy of my desires.*

11 *Every experience I have benefits me and brings me joy.*

12 *I attract all desired abundance immediately.*

MARCH

13 *My body is perfect. I am vibrant and healthy. I feel energized.*

14 *I continuously ask for what I wish to create in my life.*

15 *I look within and see the loving, beautiful being I am.*

16 *I reach all my goals easily.*

MARCH

17 *I am one-of-a-kind.*

18 *I am joyously exuberant and in harmony with all of life.*

19 God owns everything and He loves to share.

20 *I am fulfilled with my life and I show it to the world.*

MARCH

21   *I evolve, grow, and transform continuously.*

22   *I listen to my inner being.*

23   *I choose to focus only on the positive things I am creating.*

24   *My heart is wide open. Love flows through me.*

MARCH

25 *I am cheerful.*

26 *I ask continually and receive abundantly.*

27 *I feel fantastic, light, and easy.*

28 *I have creative intelligence.*

MARCH

29   *All is well all the time.*

_____
_____
_____
_____
_____

30   *I focus on the good in every moment.*

_____
_____
_____
_____
_____

31   *I am surrounded by love.*

_____
_____
_____
_____
_____

> "... with God all things are possible."
> —Matthew 19:26 (KJV)

STEP 1: CONNECT

"Seek ye **first** the Kingdom of Heaven (God) and his righteousness; and all these things shall be added unto you."
—Matthew 6:33 (KJV)

God promises us that, after we are plugged in, we receive two gifts.

First, we will receive His righteousness. This means we receive His truth and the truth shall set us free. His truth is perfection; perfection of health, wealth, relationships, and wisdom. It sets us free to live peacefully, lovingly, kindly, and joyfully as well as boldly and courageously.

The second gift we receive is "all these things shall be added" to us. What are THESE things? What THINGS? In the Holy Bible, God has left space in creation for each of us to write our own story, our own list of "things."

Let us be clear about our goals and desires for our life. Journal! Let us write every day and script our life. A life worth living is worth continual scripting.

APRIL

GRATITUDE AND BLESSINGS RECEIVED

APRIL

MONTHLY GOALS

GAINS, SUCCESSES, AND MIRACLES RECEIVED

APRIL

WEEKLY GOALS

Week 1
_____
_____
_____
_____
_____
_____

Week 2
_____
_____
_____
_____
_____
_____

Week 3
_____
_____
_____
_____
_____
_____

Week 4
_____
_____
_____
_____
_____
_____

APRIL

1 *I enjoy every day of my life.*

2 *I ask and receive all that is good.*

3 *All my organs are happy and well.*

4 *I recognize the good that is abundant everywhere.*

APRIL

5 *I am one with the present moment.*

6 *My goals are attainable.*

7 *I am happily unique.*

8 *I am thankful that God is always with me.*

APRIL

9 *I receive freely and I am a cheerful giver.*

10 *I am living a wonderful life.*

11 *I am connected to a power that is greater than my individual self.*

12 *I choose to view my world friendly.*

APRIL

13   *I focus my thoughts on what I wish to experience.*

14   *I allow my self-appreciation to increase.*

15   *It is my birthright to live joyfully and freely.*

16   *I use money to better my life and the lives of those around me.*

APRIL

17   *I meditate daily.*

18   *I have awesome potential in my life.*

19   *I am willing to flow and allow.*

20   *I listen to and speak of excellent things.*

APRIL

21 *Divine love fills me and I express kindness, tenderness, and compassion.*

22 *I know what makes me happy.*

23 *I constantly create opportunities that attract more money.*

24 *I take ownership of all the goodness in my life right now.*

APRIL

25 *I walk a good path every day.*

26 *I am peaceful and joyous.*

27 *I choose to experience a harmonious day.*

28 *I am here to love and honor myself and others.*

APRIL

29 *I receive joy.*

30 *My finances improve continually. I constantly have more and more money.*

> "Therefore I tell you, whatever you **ask** for in prayer, believe that you have **received** it, and it will be yours."
>
> —Mark 11:24 (NIV)

STEP 2: DECLARE

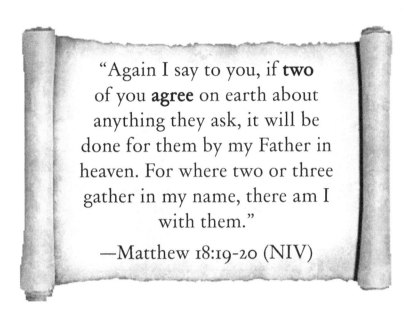

"Again I say to you, if **two** of you **agree** on earth about anything they ask, it will be done for them by my Father in heaven. For where two or three gather in my name, there am I with them."
—Matthew 18:19-20 (NIV)

Once we invite God into our heart, ask Him to stay here all day long. Let us keep our channel of communication open to Him. Once we are connected and the channel is open, we are plugged in and will continue to prosper. Now we are set up to ask and receive.

Let us check that we remain connected to God throughout the day. God is our GPS for life! We supply the address (detailed goals). He supplies the guidance and the path to achieve our destination (goals).

Let us ask by declaring our desires! As we stay in His righteousness, remember every word counts!

MAY

GRATITUDE AND BLESSINGS RECEIVED

MAY

MONTHLY GOALS

GAINS, SUCCESSES, AND MIRACLES RECEIVED

MAY

WEEKLY GOALS

Week 1

_____
_____
_____
_____
_____
_____

Week 2

_____
_____
_____
_____
_____
_____

Week 3

_____
_____
_____
_____
_____
_____

Week 4

_____
_____
_____
_____
_____
_____

MAY

1 *I open my heart and my mind to the pathway of divine energy.*

2 *I expect only great things in my life.*

3 *I meditate. Meditation is time I give myself to recharge.*

4 *I am created for success.*

MAY

5 *Individuality is a precious gift.*

6 *I always remain positive.*

7 *I am able to attract and manage large sums of money.*

8 *I love to drink water. Water serves me and I cherish it.*

MAY

9 *I attract what I constantly think about and believe to be possible.*

10 *All of me already knows how to do everything.*

11 *I am aware of the words I am using.*

12 *I know my talents and share them with the world.*

MAY

13 *My heart is always singing and dancing.*

14 *I am the co-creator of my life and the attractor of the wealth within it.*

15 *I love my body. My mind and body are in perfect balance.*

16 *I continually seize all the opportunities to improve myself.*

MAY

17 *I am joyously exuberant and in harmony with all of life.*

18 *I choose to remember only the good things.*

19 *I am amazed by how beautiful I am inside and out.*

20 *I smile, laugh, dance, and lead with my heart.*

MAY

21 *I welcome in success and my fortune with grace.*

22 *I receive inspiration, new ideas, well being, and beauty.*

23 *I have God's powerful spirit within me.*

24 *My breath is life. I inhale deeply and exhale fully.*

MAY

25 *I use the power of my words to bless myself and others.*

26 *I am a super-awesome somebody.*

27 *I have a cheerful spirit.*

28 *Money expands my experiences and offers new opportunities.*

MAY

29   *I exercise regularly. Exercise is so much fun.*

30   *Accomplished desires are sweet to the soul.*

31   *I live each day as if it is the only day of my life.*

> "**Give thanks** to the LORD, for he is **good**; his love endures forever."
>
> —Psalm 118:1 (NIV)

STEP 3: DOMINATE

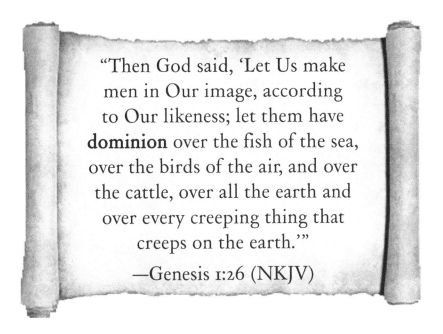

"Then God said, 'Let Us make men in Our image, according to Our likeness; let them have **dominion** over the fish of the sea, over the birds of the air, and over the cattle, over all the earth and over every creeping thing that creeps on the earth.'"
—Genesis 1:26 (NKJV)

In the first page of the Bible, God gave us dominion over the Earth. He repeated His desire for us to rule over this Earth, to show us how important this was to Him. God gave us this life to reign. We are the children of God. God delivers 100 percent of the time. With Him success is guaranteed. God shows up in a huge way. He is a miracle maker. The only way He works is supernaturally. It is our birthright to dominate. We deserve whatever good we consciously ask for.

Let us put our crown back on and the world will bow. Let us walk in our inheritance. Let us honor Him with our gracious life.

JUNE

GRATITUDE AND BLESSINGS RECEIVED

JUNE

MONTHLY GOALS

_____
_____
_____
_____
_____
_____
_____
_____
_____
_____
_____
_____
_____
_____

GAINS, SUCCESSES, AND MIRACLES RECEIVED

_____
_____
_____
_____
_____
_____
_____
_____
_____
_____
_____
_____

JUNE

WEEKLY GOALS

Week 1
_____
_____
_____
_____
_____
_____

Week 2
_____
_____
_____
_____
_____
_____

Week 3
_____
_____
_____
_____
_____
_____

Week 4
_____
_____
_____
_____
_____
_____

JUNE

1 *I keep my thoughts on the truth.*

2 *My love is like a beautiful rainbow that covers the whole sky.*

3 *My mind is happy.*

4 *I am wealthy. I am rich. I am happy.*

JUNE

5 *Being active brings me joy. I am active throughout the day.*

6 *I live up to my potential and beyond.*

7 *I continue to embrace the flow of life and this flow leads me to happiness.*

8 *I choose to do good for he who does good is of God.*

JUNE

9   *Divine love is the essence of every person.*

10   *My smile lights up the Universe.*

11   *Money comes to me easily.*

12   *I radiate with health.*

JUNE

13 *I am calm. I have a peaceful heart.*

___

14 *My positive thoughts and blessed words are magnetic, creative, and draw greatness to me.*

___

15 *By faith I declare all my actions before I take them.*

___

16 *I am worthy. I deserve.*

JUNE

17   *I am rejoicing and celebrate my well being.*

18   *I think abundantly.*

19   *My nose smells the beauty of nature.*

20   *I live creatively.*

JUNE

21 *I remain in peaceful harmony.*

22 *I write down what I welcome in each day.*

23 *Love flows through me and touches everyone in my life.*

24 *I am glad I rejoice in all.*

JUNE

25 *I am a money magnet.*

26 *My mouth smiles and speaks blessings.*

27 *I see my desires clearly. I now create the life of my dreams.*

28 *I choose to focus only on my breath for it is my gift from God.*

JUNE

29   *All the words from my mouth come forth with righteousness.*

_____
_____
_____
_____
_____

30   *I have beauty and depth within me.*

_____
_____
_____
_____
_____

> "In the beginning was the word. And the word was with God and the **word** was God."
>
> —John 1:1 (NIV)

STEP 4: BE CALM – ALIGN YOUR HEAD WITH YOUR HEART

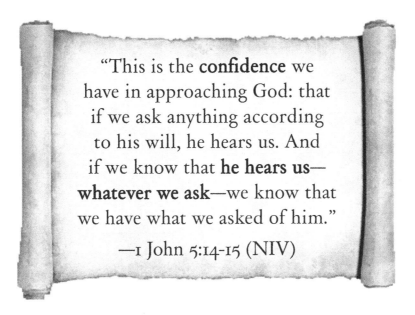

"This is the **confidence** we have in approaching God: that if we ask anything according to his will, he hears us. And if we know that **he hears us—whatever we ask**—we know that we have what we asked of him."

—1 John 5:14-15 (NIV)

In order to attract or manifest, the calmer we are and the more peace we welcome into our life, the easier things flow toward us. The more peaceful and calm we are, the more we increase our ability to receive.

Let us be in a relaxed state to recognize and receive our blessings. Let us align our emotions with our desired feelings, allowing both to head in the same direction. We know what is right for us.

Let us stay true to our righteous gut feelings. Let us find our true North and head in that direction. Let us choose to develop a clear awareness by paying renewed attention to our gut. Relax, let go, and let God embrace us. Be in peace. All is well.

JULY

GRATITUDE AND BLESSINGS RECEIVED

JULY

MONTHLY GOALS

_____
_____
_____
_____
_____
_____
_____
_____
_____
_____
_____
_____
_____
_____

GAINS, SUCCESSES, AND MIRACLES RECEIVED

_____
_____
_____
_____
_____
_____
_____
_____
_____
_____
_____
_____

JULY

WEEKLY GOALS

Week 1

Week 2

Week 3

Week 4

JULY

1 *I am truth. I am the child of God. God's goodness is in and around me always.*

2 *I am worthy of having it all. I am open to receive all the wealth life offers me.*

3 *My bones are firm yet flexible.*

4 *I am strong in the grace that is from Christ Jesus.*

JULY

5 *I flow with life and experience harmony.*

6 *I am inspired by the spirit of success as it breathes new life into my goals and desires.*

7 *I welcome pure love into my heart.*

8 *Each day is satisfying, happy, and joyous.*

JULY

9 *Prosperity is drawn to me.*

10 *My blood is clean and flows perfectly.*

11 *I am the co-creative power in my world.*

12 *I align my head with my heart.*

JULY

13 *My positive thoughts attract my desired results.*

14 *Loving is a part of who I am.*

15 *Today, I find a hundred reasons to feel good.*

16 *Money comes to me in expected and new exciting ways.*

JULY

17 *My mind is clear and I have a fantastic memory.*

18 *I continually create good in my life.*

19 *I am filled with awe and wonder.*

20 *I know that my inheritance is there for me to use and do great things with it.*

JULY

21 *The love I have for myself grows every day.*

22 *My eyes see the glory of God.*

23 *I welcome money and prosperity in my life in every moment.*

24 *I take time to be quiet and feel the presence of God.*

JULY

25 *Every step I take along the way allows me to grow.*

26 *All my decisions stem from faith.*

27 *I speak only beautiful words that create and bless.*

28 *My heart loves continuously.*

JULY

29 *I understand the Almighty Power.*

30 *New money making opportunities appear every day.*

31 *I understand that water is the source of life and I can imprint it with loving and beautiful messages.*

> "The Spirit himself testifies with our spirit that we are God's children."
> —Romans 8:16 (NIV)

STEP 5: TAKE ACTION – FOCUS ON YOUR BREATH

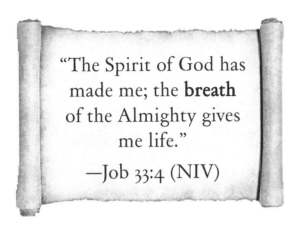

"The Spirit of God has made me; the **breath** of the Almighty gives me life."

—Job 33:4 (NIV)

Every loving aligned action taken to bless and be blessed through word or deed is the perfect action.

Just breathe; all that is required is to be calm and to breathe. This calming motion helps regain neutrality.

Let us be aware of our breath in the moment. Let us take three deep breaths and focus only on our inhalation and our exhalation.

God is in our breath. God gave us the breath of life as our first gift. God is with us now in each breath and He is with us only now, because there only is now.

Let us focus on our breath, relax our breathing, smile and keep calm, let it go, and let life flow.

AUGUST

GRATITUDE AND BLESSINGS RECEIVED

AUGUST

MONTHLY GOALS

___

GAINS, SUCCESSES, AND MIRACLES RECEIVED

___

AUGUST

WEEKLY GOALS

Week 1
_____
_____
_____
_____
_____
_____

Week 2
_____
_____
_____
_____
_____
_____

Week 3
_____
_____
_____
_____
_____
_____

Week 4
_____
_____
_____
_____
_____
_____

AUGUST

1 *I ask more to receive more.*

2 *I am blessed with joy and love.*

3 *I choose to see the highest good in everyone.*

4 *I am filled with love and gratitude.*

AUGUST

5 *My joy expands me and aligns me with God.*

6 *I am mentally and emotionally able to enjoy a loving, prosperous life.*

7 *I feel amazing as I experience my sweet and joyous life.*

8 *I take responsibility for all my creations.*

AUGUST

9   *I am alive to experience God's greatness.*

10   *I am completely focused.*

11   *I love myself so that I can love others.*

12   *I am joyous and I believe.*

AUGUST

13   *I give myself permission to be very rich.*

14   *I am who I choose to be right now.*

15   *I encourage my desires and let my creative juices flow into everything I choose to do.*

16   *I embrace all the wonder the Universe has to offer.*

AUGUST

17 *I declare the exact outcome for all my actions.*

18 *I love all humanity.*

19 *I have faith. I believe. My heart is at peace.*

20 *I feel good about money.*

AUGUST

21   *I am perfect exactly as I am right now.*

22   *I love to travel and experience the world.*

23   *I greet each day with excitement.*

24   *I reach my desires fast, accurately, and easily.*

AUGUST

25   *I have great appreciation for everyone and everything in my life.*

26   *In Christ all things are possible.*

27   *I only think and speak positively about money.*

28   *I am my best friend and the person I enjoy being with the most.*

AUGUST

29   *I live my divine purpose.*

---

30   *I feel blessed.*

---

31   *I have clarity and focus on all I do today.*

> "I came that they may **have life**, and have it **abundantly**."
> —John 10:10 (ESV)

STEP 6: LEAD WITH LOVE – LET US LOVE OURSELVES FIRST

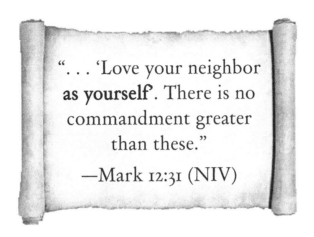

"... 'Love your neighbor **as yourself**'. There is no commandment greater than these."
—Mark 12:31 (NIV)

After fulfilling the first commandment, let us concentrate on the second one. Love yourself first in order to love others.

Let us start practicing being alone with God in joy. Let us be comfortable with ourselves. Let us feel good about ourselves. The more we love ourselves, the friendlier our world becomes. Let us love ourselves with grace. We are our own most critical judges. Instead, let us be our biggest fans. We have to cheer for ourselves. Go me! Go me!

Remember, we are exactly where we are meant to be in every moment.

SEPTEMBER

GRATITUDE AND BLESSINGS RECEIVED

SEPTEMBER

MONTHLY GOALS

GAINS, SUCCESSES, AND MIRACLES RECEIVED

SEPTEMBER

WEEKLY GOALS

Week 1

Week 2

Week 3

Week 4

SEPTEMBER

1 *I have great plans for my life and I write them down.*

2 *Today the love in me overflows and I create a beautiful, loving world.*

3 *I am in my perfect place and God cheers me on.*

4 *I clearly see light and easy ways to make money.*

SEPTEMBER

5 *I experience healing energy in my entire body.*

6 *God's divine energy lifts me up.*

7 *I appreciate the blessing each new moment brings.*

8 *I am clear about what I intend for each day.*

SEPTEMBER

9 *My love is so great that it surrounds all.*

10 *I am responsible for all the happiness in my life.*

11 *I receive financial abundance by being who I am.*

12 *Today I am an energetic, productive, happy being.*

SEPTEMBER

13 *I live in the light.*

14 *I am understanding.*

15 *I ask for my desires with great precision. I love to declare in exact detail.*

16 *I see only the good in myself and others.*

SEPTEMBER

17 *I am one with the very Power that created me.*

18 *My actions attract constant prosperity.*

19 *I am relaxed.*

20 *All creative thoughts manifest in wonderful ways.*

SEPTEMBER

21 *I look up and let the sun shine on my face.*

22 *I have the power to welcome only the thoughts that bless me. I have the power to turn away all opposing thoughts.*

23 *I share perfect love and in return I receive perfect love.*

24 *I trust in the Lord with all my heart.*

SEPTEMBER

25 *I embrace new avenues of income.*

26 *I believe in myself.*

27 *I expand with all the experiences I welcome in throughout my day.*

28 *All life exists within me.*

SEPTEMBER

29   *I declare all of my desires in writing.*

30   *I am God's beautiful creation.*

> "Be careful how you think; your life is shaped by your thoughts."
> —Proverbs 4:23 (GNT)

STEP 7: BLESS EVERYONE AND EVERYTHING WITH LOVE AND GRATITUDE

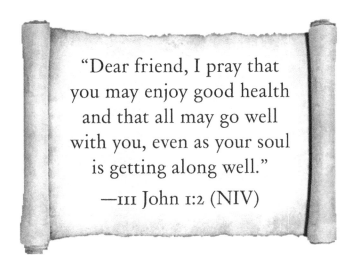

"Dear friend, I pray that you may enjoy good health and that all may go well with you, even as your soul is getting along well."

—III John 1:2 (NIV)

When we decide to focus on love and gratitude, it immediately changes our emotional state. When we decide to look at every event or person with love and gratitude, our feelings toward them can only be positive. Love everyone and everything with love and gratitude. Allow everyone to be just as they are and everything just as it is.

Praise God for the perfection it all is. God believes in us; let us believe in each other's perfection. Have mercy on each other, trusting that we will all grow into our own greatness.

With our kind words and positive intentions our world has the opportunity to be transformed into a kind, loving, friendly place.

OCTOBER

GRATITUDE AND BLESSINGS RECEIVED

OCTOBER

MONTHLY GOALS

_____
_____
_____
_____
_____
_____
_____
_____
_____
_____
_____
_____
_____
_____
_____

GAINS, SUCCESSES, AND MIRACLES RECEIVED

_____
_____
_____
_____
_____
_____
_____
_____
_____
_____
_____
_____
_____
_____

OCTOBER

WEEKLY GOALS

Week 1

_____
_____
_____
_____
_____
_____

Week 2

_____
_____
_____
_____
_____
_____

Week 3

_____
_____
_____
_____
_____
_____

Week 4

_____
_____
_____
_____
_____
_____

OCTOBER

1 *I prepare my day with joy and exuberance.*

2 *I enjoy receiving money.*

3 *I always see myself at my best.*

4 *I grow as I align with God.*

OCTOBER

5 *The calm, happy, gentle peace alive in me brings me comfort, solace, and joy.*

6 *My goals are exciting and I achieve them light and easy.*

7 *I am proud of my self-image.*

8 *My connection to God grows stronger every day.*

OCTOBER

9 *Every day I am receiving more and more wealth.*

10 *I enjoy eating nutritious food.*

11 *I am the author of my own life.*

12 *I experience peace today and every day.*

OCTOBER

13   *I visualize myself achieving all my goals.*

14   *I am a shining star in this dazzling world.*

15   *Every day I do something that is fun for me.*

16   *I am open to receive lots of money right now.*

OCTOBER

17 *Walking barefoot keeps me grounded.*

18 *I actively create the life I wish to live.*

19 *I take ownership of my life right now.*

20 *I know that my thoughts attract and my words create everything.*

OCTOBER

21 *We are all children of God and I choose to respect God by showing love, compassion, and understanding to myself and others.*

___

22 *God is good all the time.*

___

23 *I receive abundant blessings.*

___

24 *My healthy body serves me well.*

OCTOBER

25 *I understand that my life's path is up to me.*

26 *I feel amazing as I experience my sweet and joyful life.*

27 *I achieve whatever I focus on.*

28 *I love and respect myself.*

OCTOBER

29 *God supports me.*

---

30 *I always prosper in everything I do.*

---

31 *Water assists me with my well being.*

> "... For the mouth speaks what the heart is full of."
> —Luke 6:45 (NIV)

STEP 8: EXPECT THE MIRACLE IN EVERY MOMENT

"Trust in the LORD with all your heart and lean not on your own understanding; in all your ways **submit to him**, and he will make your paths straight."
—Proverbs 3:5-6 (NIV)

The truth is, this whole life is miraculous.

If we order online and we click on express checkout, we expect the delivery to come the next day and we happily wait for our package at the front door with full confidence. How fast do we expect our delivery from the Universe, the most perfect delivery system of all time?

It is up to us to recreate the expectation that miracles are available to us in every moment. Life is a series of choices. Let us choose to see everything as the miracle it is. In Christ all things are possible. If we choose to live our lives seeking and expecting miracles in our daily walk, we will recognize them everywhere.

NOVEMBER

GRATITUDE AND BLESSINGS RECEIVED

NOVEMBER

MONTHLY GOALS

GAINS, SUCCESSES, AND MIRACLES RECEIVED

NOVEMBER

WEEKLY GOALS

Week 1

_____
_____
_____
_____
_____
_____

Week 2

_____
_____
_____
_____
_____
_____

Week 3

_____
_____
_____
_____
_____
_____

Week 4

_____
_____
_____
_____
_____
_____

NOVEMBER

1   *I embrace all experiences with love, wisdom, and gratitude.*

2   *I am alive, aware, joyous, and enthusiastic about life.*

3   *My clear thoughts and written declarations help me to achieve whatever I desire.*

4   *I love from a pure heart, from a good conscience, and from sincere faith.*

NOVEMBER

5 *Wonderful things keep happening to me.*

6 *I claim my divine inheritance.*

7 *My active body is transformed with my conscious mind.*

8 *I am open and flexible. I encourage change.*

NOVEMBER

9 *My life is fantastic, accomplished, and filled with joyful freedom.*

10 *Focusing on my joyful thoughts creates my joyful world.*

11 *I forgive myself. I love myself.*

12 *To God be the glory.*

NOVEMBER

13 *I feel rich and blessed.*

14 *I always feel youthful.*

15 *God gave me dominion over this earth.*

16 *I always am my best.*

NOVEMBER

17 *I focus on positive thoughts, because the thoughts I think attract. I focus on speaking positive words, because the words I speak create.*

18 *The smile on my face expresses the love in my heart.*

19 *I give thanks for each new day.*

20 *I am receiving multiple streams of income.*

NOVEMBER

21   *I feel energized.*

22   *I am conscious of the words I speak.*

23   *I happily flow and evolve with beautiful inspiration.*

24   *I only speak kind and positive words.*

NOVEMBER

25 *I love myself for the awesome being that I am.*

---

26 *I am created in God's image.*

---

27 *God has plans to prosper me.*

---

28 *I truly love nature. I find beauty everywhere.*

NOVEMBER

29   *I understand that I am in co-creation with God.*

30   *I pay attention to my breath.*

> "Let your **conversation** be **gracious** and **attractive** so that you will have the right response for everyone."
>
> —Colossians 4:6 (NLT)

STEP 9: HAVE FUN AND CELEBRATE

"Rejoice in the Lord **always**: and again I say, **Rejoice**."
—Philippians 4:4 (KJV)

Let us live every moment in the present and ask ourselves how we can celebrate our life in this moment. There is only the present moment. Life was given to us to live it abundantly, to celebrate with the heart of a child, and have fun. Let us enjoy our life experiences in a childlike state.

Let us make sure that we remember to laugh like children all the time. Laughter inspires hope and forgiveness. The happier our attitude and the more we smile and laugh, the healthier our minds and bodies are. Let us allow ourselves to have fun. Let us rejoice always!

DECEMBER

GRATITUDE AND BLESSINGS RECEIVED

_____
_____
_____
_____
_____
_____
_____
_____
_____
_____
_____
_____
_____
_____
_____
_____
_____
_____
_____
_____
_____
_____
_____
_____
_____
_____
_____
_____
_____

DECEMBER

MONTHLY GOALS

GAINS, SUCCESSES, AND MIRACLES RECEIVED

DECEMBER

WEEKLY GOALS

Week 1

_____
_____
_____
_____
_____
_____

Week 2

_____
_____
_____
_____
_____
_____

Week 3

_____
_____
_____
_____
_____
_____

Week 4

_____
_____
_____
_____
_____
_____

DECEMBER

1 *Everything I write down I edit three times to make sure I create what I prefer most.*

2 *Because I come from love, I am love.*

3 *I hear the voice of God.*

4 *I welcome continual income and wealth in my life.*

DECEMBER

5 *I actively participate in my life.*

6 *I am the co-creator of my life. I share in God's creation power.*

7 *My life dances with excitement.*

8 *With the help of my journal I organize my thoughts.*

DECEMBER

9 *I allow my self-appreciation to increase daily.*

10 *I rejoice always, and again I say rejoice.*

11 *I only think positive thoughts about money, prosperity, and abundance.*

12 *I ask for God's blessing before I eat my food.*

DECEMBER

13 *I create my perfect life every day.*

_____
_____
_____
_____
_____

14 *I am alive and free to be the highest version of me.*

_____
_____
_____
_____
_____

15 *I can feel the perfection of my choices. I am always on my direct path.*

_____
_____
_____
_____
_____

16 *I have abundant love in my life.*

_____
_____
_____
_____
_____

DECEMBER

17 *All happiness starts within.*

18 *I continually attract more success and fulfillment.*

19 *My clear thinking and happy thoughts turn into a joyful performance each day.*

20 *I receive whatever I desire immediately.*

DECEMBER

21 *My life is balanced and flows light and easy.*

___

22 *I align with a prayer partner who encourages me and seconds my asking.*

___

23 *I love God and God loves me.*

___

24 *I am deeply fulfilled by all that I am.*

___

DECEMBER

25 *I believe in the absolute prosperity and abundance of God.*

26 *I breathe deeply and fully.*

27 *I am grateful and ready to live my day.*

28 *It is natural for me to feel good and be well.*

DECEMBER

29   *My conscious thoughts and beautiful words plant the seeds of success.*

---

30   *I am love and light.*

---

31   *Now is an awesome opportunity for a new beginning.*

> "This is the day that the Lord has made; let us rejoice and be glad in it."
>
> —Psalm 118:24 (ESV)

Notes

Notes

Notes

Notes

Notes

Notes

Notes

Notes

Notes

Notes

Notes

Dear Father God,

You are the light of my life.
Thank You for this perfect day.
Thank You for this perfect moment.

Thank You for creating me in Your image.
I accept that I am Your child and that
I hold Your creation power.

Thank You for Your wisdom.
Thank You for allowing me plenty of time
to accomplish everything.
Most of all, I am thankful that You are always with me
and are my greatest support.

My life is balanced and flows light and easy.
I recognize the good that is abundant everywhere.

I am calm. I have a peaceful heart.

I am Love.
I love myself so that I can have love for others.
I find it easy to love myself and others.
Love flows through me and touches everyone in my life.

My love is so great that it surrounds all and everything.
I constantly create great thoughts of love and joy.

I am joy. I am a true blessing.
Keep me cheerful so that I may serve You.

I am grateful that I know the truth.
I am grateful that I have a definite life's purpose.

I am grateful that I use beautiful positive words that create.
It is my intention to speak with clarity, happiness, and love.
May every thought I think and every word I speak be
full of Your perfect love.

I am grateful that I am incredibly successful and
that wealth and abundance come from everywhere.
Money flows frequently and abundantly.

I rejoice in You Jesus.

With love, gratitude and happiness,

Your loving child

AVAILABLE FROM RECEIVE JOY

ASK AND YOU SHALL RECEIVE

The Power of Positive Words
+ the Law of Attraction
+ God
= Your Light and Easy Life!

This is "the secret beyond the secret"! This book will help encourage you to create and define a direction and plan for your life. I wish to share my Nine Step Method to empower everyone to feel the freedom of a light and easy life. Open your heart and your mind and journey with me to a new and more powerful, focused and loved, aware and connected You.

$15 (Amazon $20)
ISBN: 978-0-9988484-8-8

ASK AND YOU SHALL RECEIVE MEDITATION

Enjoy this 20-minute *Ask And You Shall Receive Meditation* in all positive words—listen to the truth about yourself and receive inspiration.

$5
UPC: 098867225629

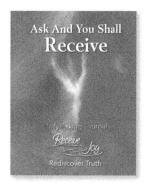

DAILY ASKING JOURNAL
Live by Design!

To make your life light and easy, let us put the Nine Step Method into daily action by using the *Daily Asking Journal*. This Journal will help connect you with the Power of the Universe and enable you to collect and compile all your asking intentions in one place. This personal journal for your focused thoughts and positive words supports you to raise your awareness, while having an organized platform to consciously create and record your positive, happy, light, and easy life. Script your life, keep on asking God, and be a new wineskin.

$10 (Amazon $12)
ISBN: 978-0-9988484-0-2

CONNECT TO THE LIGHT

We charge our cellphone, plug in the toaster and the hairdryer, let us also plug our life in first. Step one in the process of truly deciding to make changes in our life and begin living by design starts with the understanding that we are connected to the greatest Power Source there is—God. Let us consciously connect first and harness this power. Once we are connected, our life starts to flow.

Connect To The Light provides ways to maintain our connection to the light energy and to live by conscious design. Let us be heavenly-minded, yet of earthly use.

$20 (Amazon $20)
ISBN: 978-0-9988484-1-9

FOCUS WHEEL WORKBOOK

The *Focus Wheel Workbook* presents you with an easy exercise to engage your belief system, stay in a positive mindset, and pray into the solution. Receive Joy collected over 50 statements to help you think about excellent and praiseworthy things. Encourage yourself to increase your belief in all areas of life by expressing clarity and solid evidence in writing. This workbook also aids in believing in and focusing on your goals. Seek God first, focus on your greatness, and live by design.

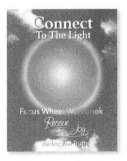

$15 (Amazon $20)
ISBN: 978-0-9988484-9-5

RECEIVE INSPIRATION

Receive Inspiration contains a mix of inspirations to open the mind to receive happiness, love, prosperity, well-being, growth, focus, and allowing. Receive Joy created this encouraging CD using only positive words that we may consciously choose to remember our greatness. Let us cheer ourselves on! Be inspired!

CD, $10
UPC. 098867227227

RECEIVE BEAUTIFUL WORDS

Every word is a creation. We can choose to create love, joy, gratitude, hope, compassion, mercy, praise and much more positivity with our words. Let us be conscious of which word we send out to achieve what we desire. Play *Receive Beautiful Words* to imprint ourselves and our environment with positive blessings. Listen and Receive Joy!

CD, $10
UPC: 098867227128

Receive Joy

Rediscover Truth

To learn more visit **www.receivejoy.com**

Subscribe to our newsletter to continue your receiving of positive awareness. Please share your email address with us. Send us a message or directly to **ask@receivejoy.com**

Call or text to U.S. cell phone number **(239) 450-1240**

Like and follow Receive Joy on Facebook:
www.facebook.com/ReceiveJoy

Follow Receive Joy on Instagram:
@receivejoy #receivejoy

We are happy to hear from you and receive your positive feedback, inspiration, and miracle stories!

With Love and Gratitude,

Receive Joy ♡

Made in United States
Orlando, FL
20 July 2024

49329690R10102